Seeking First the Kingdom

SEEKING FIRST THE KINGDOM

Called to Faithful Stewardship

Robert A. Yoder

Foreword by Gordon Zook

HERALD PRESS
Scottdale, Pennsylvania
Kitchener, Ontario
1983

Library of Congress Cataloging in Publication Data

Yoder, Robert A., 1926-
  Seeking first the kingdom.

  Bibliography: p.
  1. Stewardship, Christian.   I. Title.
BV772.Y62   1983   248'.6   83-16618
ISBN 0-8361-3349-8 (pbk.)

SEEKING FIRST THE KINGDOM
Copyright © 1983 by Herald Press, Scottdale, Pa. 15683
  Published simultaneously in Canada by Herald Press,
  Kitchener, Ont. N2G 4M5
Library of Congress Catalog Card Number: 83-16618
International Standard Book Number: 0-8361-3349-8
Printed in the United States of America
Design by Alice B. Shetler

83 84 85 86 87 88 10 9 8 7 6 5 4 3 2 1

To my wife, Doris,
our children and their spouses
—Michael and Carolyn
—Sue and Cecil
—Dan and Donna
—and Erik
these words are dedicated
as an affirmation of Psalm 100:5.

Contents

Foreword by Gordon Zook 9
Author's Preface 13

1 God's People in the Middle 17
   Perspective
   Revelation 1:4-8

2 The Holy Disturbance 23
   Faith and economics, a North American dilemma
   Matthew 6:19-34

3 Ever Since Babel 30
   Learning, knowledge, technology
   Genesis 11:1-7

4 Dominion: Owners or Managers? .38
   Ecology, conservation, limits
   Psalm 8

5 Settled People in Unsettled Times 46
   History and experience, Mennos and economics
   Deuteronomy 8:10-20

6 Mennonites and Money: Resources or Charity? 57
   Stewardship options and models
   Luke 12:22-34

7 Facing the Future....................................70
    Dealing faithfully with change
    1 Peter 4:7-11

Appendices
    A. "A Call to Faithful Stewardship," from Mennonite
       Church General Board to all members of the
       Mennonite Church 79
    B. "Christian Stewardship: The Real World,"
       by John H. Rudy 83
    C. "When the Big House Is Full,"
       by Arnold W. Cressman 85

References Cited....................................93
Bibliography 95
The Author 101

Foreword

Since 1977 Robert Yoder has talked about stewardship in almost every conference of the Mennonite Church. As a part-time staff person for the Mennonite Board of Congregational Ministries (MBCM), he devotes summers and winters to expanding stewardship vision across the continent. In the spring he plants corn and soybeans on the family farm near Eureka, Illinois, and in the fall he stays home for the harvest.

From his earliest years in farming, Bob has been active in soil and conservation projects. In 1965 he became president of the newly merged Farmers Grain Cooperative of Eureka, relinquishing the position in 1977 to work with MBCM. In 1968 *Prairie Farmer* magazine named Bob an Illinois Master Farmer in recognition of his efforts in conservation and as a community leader.

Bob has been a member of the Roanoke Mennonite Church since his confession of faith and baptism as a youth. Although not an ordained minister, his ministry in the congregation and wider church has been extensive. He has served regularly as a congregational elder. He served as vice-president of the Illinois Mennonite Con-

ference from 1970 to 1975 and as a two-term member of
the Goshen College Board of Overseers from 1972 to
1980. In 1982 he was elected president of the Illinois
Mennonite Conference. As MBCM secretary for stewardship, he serves as a member of the Stewardship Task
Force of the Mennonite Church General Board.

In the seven chapters of this book Bob sets forth the
essence of what he has been sharing across the continent.
He has presented his messages in conference sessions, in
business retreats, in congregational settings, and in pas-
toral groups. While most hearers have been Mennonites,
he has also addressed a Faith and Agriculture conference
of the Evangelical Covenant Church of North America
and other denominational groups.

The bibliography at the end of the book indicates
references which have stimulated Bob's thinking. He lists
these in addition to the central influence: the Bible. Bob
has done a remarkable job of bridging the conversation
between thinkers and doers—both in teaching and modeling stewardship.

Most clearly, Bob's speaking and writing reflect the
reality of the struggle—the "holy disturbance" he calls
it—of being both businessman and Christian, entrepreneur and disciple, citizen of this world and of the
kingdom which is coming. While his illustrations are
drawn from the arenas he knows best, Bob's insights have
much broader application. You don't need to be a farmer
or businessperson or a Mennonite to sense the challenge.
You do, however, need to be committed to Jesus, affirm-
ing that the kingdom we seek is the Lord's and not our
own.

I am delighted that Bob Yoder's message is available
for the many who have not previously had opportunity to

interact with him. Those who have heard him will appreciate this more permanent record of Bob's clear and incisive voice. I trust that individual readers of this book and persons in study groups will find new insight, conviction, and courage to walk as stewards of Jesus Christ.

Gordon Zook, Executive Secretary
Mennonite Board of Congregational Ministries
Elkhart, Indiana
April 1983

_____ Author's Preface _____

"Here's seventeen dollars, dad. Since I won't be in church at Roanoke next Sunday, would you drop it in the offering plate for me?" Erik was busily finishing the last-minute packing details before leaving the country for a three-month study-service trimester in Costa Rica with other students from Goshen College.

Several days later I looked at the check lying there on my desk: "Pay to the order of Roanoke Mennonite Church—Seventeen and no/100 dollars." The money itself would make scant difference in the church budget dollar for dollar. Certainly the local congregation, Illinois Mennonite Conference, and the churchwide agencies would all eventually receive a share, but most importantly, the check represented an expression of faith and commitment. It was given to the one who calls all of his followers to "seek first the kingdom of God and his righteousness." It was a tithe of a larger sum that had been earned.

The gift showed me that my son had accepted a deep belief about stewardship. The happy emotion that swept over me in contemplation of this act of faith called to

mind the early stewardship teaching I had received from
my own parents and grandmother.

Stewardship is a way of life that grows out of a faith
commitment to Jesus Christ. It is both a belief and a statement about who is in charge of one's life. The stubs of
one's checkbook reveal the answer in dollars and cents.

Archimedes declared, "Give me a solid place to stand,
and I can move the earth." Jesus Christ becomes that
solid place on which believers stand and from which we
employ the entrusted resources of time, talent, and
treasure.

Jesus' call for us to act as steward managers becomes
our priority call. Seventeen hours, minutes, or seconds of
time, seventeen cents, seventeen dollars, or seventeen
thousand dollars become expressions of stewardship when
offered as Jesus' steward manager. Without faith commitment these acts revert to the simple charity of "resound-
ing gongs or clanging cymbals," the basis for another tax
deduction.

My own experience in the economic world as an ag-
ribusinessman, and more recently as part-time staff
person with Mennonite Board of Congregational Ministries, continues to be filled with challenge and opportunity. The past thirty years in business exposed me to
times of prosperity as well as times of leanness and
recession. Double digit inflation with accompanying high
interest rates, rapidly fluctuating markets, the uncertainty
of weather, insect and weed pests, the strength of the
dollar relative to foreign currencies, and governmental
decisions beyond my control all affect the "bottom line"
of the balance sheet. Its message cannot be minimized or
ignored.

I believe, however, that it is possible to be a part of the

business world and also be a serious follower of Jesus Christ. Decisions must be made in a broader context than economics alone; they must also be made by faith. That calls forth the "holy disturbance" about which I write.

Stewardship education must be balanced between conviction and mechanics, between the *why* and the *how-to*. Conviction without practice is empty and useless, just as giving without commitment becomes an exercise in self-righteousness. I am convinced that the church will reach a new level of self-understanding and joyful purpose as we allow the Scriptures to speak afresh to our needs today.

Many of the mechanics of stewardship, the *how-to* part, can be purchased and presented in neat, correct techniques, efficiently programmed on a computer. But tax planning, fund-raising methods, and computer programs do not generate stewardship conviction although these components can and should have a legitimate place in stewardship programs. Stewardship conviction comes from a faith encounter with the living Lord who bids us to seek first the kingdom.

Faithfulness and flexibility become watchwords for stewards today. To hold fast in faithfulness to one Lord, and to move and adapt with proper flexibility in a world of accelerating changes, are challenges the steward brings to the church. And the church, under the Word of God, welcomes such stewardship as part of its mission in the world.

The pages that follow express some of my convictions about stewardship. Much of the content has been presented before various congregational and conference gatherings in the course of my teaching ministry with MBCM. Some who have especially appreciated these thoughts have been kind enough to urge me to put them in writing. I thank these persons for their interest, faith in me, and encouragement in completing this task.

For the reader who may disagree with me, whether you find the thoughts too simplistic, too pro- or too anti-business, or for whatever reason, I ask correction and the privilege to grow into new truth. I ask the same favor from the reader who concurs with the ideas expressed here. I welcome questions, counsel, and encouragement to continue to grow in my own walk of stewardship.

These words are offered for God's glory by one who believes that Christ is indeed my fulcrum, the solid ground on which I stand, and the one to whom as a steward I can commit both my "seventeen dollars" and my life with integrity.

I thank those persons who have read the manuscript and offered valuable suggestions. They have helped me be a steward of words. I am grateful especially to my wife, Doris, who has been a greater influence on our steward-ship thinking and action than these words can tell. Our children, and now our extended family, continue to provide a welcome circle in which to think steward thoughts. A note of thanks to Gordon Zook for seeing the manuscript through to the publisher, to Betty Brenneman for typing and making the corrections, and to John Bender for editing. To all these and others unnamed my sincere thanks.

Robert A. Yoder
Friedensland Farms,
Eureka, Illinois
January 1983

1. God's People in the _____ Middle _____

John,
To the seven churches in the province of Asia:
Grace and peace to you from him who is, and who was, and who is to come, and from the seven spirits before his throne, and from Jesus Christ, who is the faithful witness, the firstborn from the dead, and the ruler of the kings of the earth.

To him who loves us and has freed us from our sins by his blood, and has made us to be a kingdom and priests to serve his God and Father—to him be glory and power for ever and ever! Amen.

Look, he is coming with the clouds,
     and every eye will see him,
even those who pierced him;
     and all the peoples of the earth
          will mourn because of him.
                    So shall it be! Amen.

"I am the Alpha and the Omega," says the Lord God, "who is, and who was, and who is to come, the Almighty."
                    —*Revelation 1:4-8*

What does man gain from all his labor at which he toils under the sun?
                    —*Ecclesiastes 1:3*

17

If the dead are not raised, "Let us eat and drink, for
tomorrow we die."
—*1 Corinthians 15:32b*

Carried gently in the arms of my parents and
grandparents, and now privileged to carry my own grandchildren, I've passed through the doors of the Roanoke
Mennonite Church at least three thousand times. It really
adds up over the course of fifty-six years in the same community. How many times has it been for worship? How
often has it just been force of habit? Has it been fifty
years of a growing religious experience or one year's
experience repeated fifty times?

My Christian life as a Mennonite businessman has
been one of gradual growth, starting at the home of my
parents and grandmother. At age 12 I experienced
conversion and joined the church. Here I found nurture
from brothers and sisters and acceptance of my gifts.

In my own study of Paul Erb's book *The Alpha and the
Omega* I was introduced to the one who is, who was, and
who is to come. This Christian understanding of human
experience throughout history—beginning, middle, and
ending—enables me to believe that life is more than a
series of meaningless events of chance. I'm one of God's
people in the middle, somewhere between the beginning
and the ending. I need to be reminded of this from time
to time to keep perspectives broad, not to allow the events
of the past week to narrow my viewpoint.

To understand God's working in the world, one needs
to look beyond one's own lifespan and the times in which
one lives. The story of God's people as told in the Scriptures shows that events of history placed the faithful ones
in varied situations. These ranged from the times of blessing and plenty experienced by David and his peers,

where the people surely said, "God is good—we are blessed," to the times of Daniel and Ezekiel when the people lived captive in a strange land.

Is God sweet or is God bitter? I ponder this as a rich North American who has lived all of his life in a free country, enjoying the fruits of an affluent culture in which my denomination is accepting without much question many of the values of the larger society. My North American filter clouds the universal message of the Bible. Try as I might, my cultural baggage influences how I understand the Scriptures. If God's Word is true it must be just as true in South America, or Africa, as it is in central Illinois. God's Word is true and universal, and that should raise questions for me about how I understand it and the circumstances in which I live.

What does it mean to be one of God's people in the middle, in a world rapidly becoming urban, with more than 65 percent of all Christians living in the Southern Hemisphere, cut off from much of the affluence and wealth that I am tempted to say is mine? Am I blessed because I'm good, or was I born at a time in history in which circumstances have given me advantages never dreamed of by others? How can I respond faithfully to God?

How do my brothers and sisters in the Third World, living in poverty and oppression, understand the biblical verses that speak of blessings, abundance, and thankfulness? Surely we North Americans must listen to them in their understanding of God's universal Word. Listening will make me vulnerable and may well cause a rethinking about what church really means. The Lord is teaching me that the church knows no national boundary and that the church cannot be captive to any economic or political system.

There is no Christian economic system. Every system must stand under the judgment and scrutiny of God. Each system has its own unique set of problems. Even as Christians are called to live and work in the real world where we are, we must first attempt to relate to our communities, nations, and universe as members of God's kingdom. That loyalty transcends all others. Christians are called to faithfulness as first fruit models of the kingdom of God, living in expectation of the kingdom yet to come with all its promised blessings.

Being God's people in the middle has yet another dimension which takes on the form of a squeeze—finding ourselves "between a rock and a hard place." Paul calls it "being conformed to the world" (Rom. 12:2). J. B. Phillips calls it allowing "the world to squeeze [us] . . . into its own mold," rather than letting "God remold [our] . . . minds from within."

Mennonites have a word for it, too: nonconformity. How I've fought and struggled with that word. During my teenage years of carelessness and rebellion, I hated that word with all my being, for it stood for much of what I wanted to throw off. Why should I be different in looks or actions from anyone else? Why not allow myself to be "one of the boys?"

Now, more than ever, I have come to believe that the church today, Mennonites included, urgently needs to redefine and rediscover real nonconformity. The pressure to conform is tremendous. Each time we open a magazine, pick up the newspaper, turn on the television, there it is—the squeeze of the world, the force of our technological society forming and conforming our minds. We dare not abandon ourselves to the mass-mind of pseudo-needs and pseudo-satisfactions, that is, take our values from the many powerful secular forces swirling daily about us. God waits to mold our minds.

Jesus calls us the "little flock." Sociologists would call us a cognitive minority, a group of people who hold a set of beliefs that differ sharply from the majority in their society. Just when many Mennonites are breathing a sigh of relief that we are not perceived as all that different anymore, I'm convinced that now, more than ever, we need to be different in the right ways and for the right reasons. Our attitudes as Christians are formed by Jesus Christ, our Savior and Lord.

My perspectives have become clearer; being one of God's people in the middle gives a sense of understanding to the past, present, and future. It also sharpens the focus of the present struggle to be salt and light, a city set on a hill, as Jesus said, in the world but not of the world. I venture into today concerned about the conditions on our planet and uneasy about my contribution to a misapplication of the Scriptures which interprets them as speaking only to the feeding and satisfying of the mind, heart, and spirit. At the bottom of it all, however, I ask God to use this imperfect yet renewed vessel to live in this day, in this middle hour, the victory and mission that is mine.

Time for Reflection

1. What do you think stewardship means? Tell the person next to you.
2. To what extent does your definition of stewardship include God, other Christians, and other parts of your religious faith?
3. How would your definition of Christian stewardship be

understood by (a) members of your local congregation, (b) Christians in the Third World, (c) your non-Christian neighbors and friends? What parts would each group find hard to understand?

4. In what ways are your beliefs about stewardship different from (a) your non-Christian neighbors and friends, (b) the norms of your community, (c) other Christians in your community?

5. What recent experience have you had of living in the middle? How is God conforming your mind on the matter?

6. Why do you think the author says there is no Christian economic system?

2. The Holy Disturbance

Do not store up for yourselves treasures on earth, where moth and rust destroy, and where thieves break in and steal. But store up for yourselves treasures in heaven, where moth and rust do not destroy, and where thieves do not break in and steal. For where your treasure is, there your heart will be also.

The eye is the lamp of the body. If your eyes are good, your whole body will be full of light. But if your eyes are bad, your whole body will be full of darkness. If then the light within you is darkness, how great is that darkness!

No one can serve two masters. Either he will hate the one and love the other, or he will be devoted to the one and despise the other. You cannot serve both God and Money.

—Matthew 6:19-24

This [present] level of money raising for only a small part of the total institutional life of North American Mennonite churches is possible only in denominations which have successful farmers and prosperous businessmen, active in the marketplace, striving to expand, eager to innovate, always dissatisfied with present sales and service.

—Donovan Smucker, 1976:228°

°Page references throughout are given parenthetically in the text. See "References Cited" for other related information.

If all the light you have is darkness, it is dark indeed!
—*Matthew 6:23b, Phillips*

It's all there in front of me on a neat computer printout—an analysis of our farm business for the past year. The results reflect hours of toil and sweat, decisions both good and bad, double digit inflation, high interest rates, rapidly fluctuating markets affected by weather, politics, and world events beyond my control. I am reminded again of the prayers we offered at planting and harvest time. Thoughts of faith and economics revolve in my mind. Are the two really like oil and water, un-mixable?

Since 1951, I've looked at yearly analyses like this one, although they have not always been computerized. Analysis figures, while impersonal, give important and re-vealing information, such as feed and grain returns per tillable acre, seed and crop expense, depreciation, crop yields, and selling price. All these data blend together to disclose farm and family earnings, management returns, and rate earned on investment. The facts disclosed can only be ignored at the risk of business stagnation or failure. My banker tells me, "It's what's on the bottom line that counts, Bob."

The teachings of Jesus lie before me, too—even the tough ones such as Matthew 6:24: "No one can serve two masters. Either he will hate the one and love the other, or he will be devoted to the one and despise the other. You cannot serve both God and Money."

This gives hardworking, energetic, success-oriented businesspersons a real problem. How does one reckon with the teachings of Jesus concerning economics? How can I take seriously his words about not being anxious, not laying up treasures on earth, remembering the Sabbath, giving money away, and leaving all to follow him? Jesus also says, "It's what's on the bottom line that counts, Bob." The bottom line, I believe, is faithfulness for one who would follow Jesus.

But how can one put together economic reality and the call of Jesus for undivided loyalty and faithfulness? It is where faith and economics meet that the *holy disturbance* takes place. For one who takes seriously economic reality and faithfulness to Christ the answers are neither obvious or easy. Those who would offer simple answers to complex problems should be reminded that perhaps they haven't thought of all of the questions.

Jesus stands before us; his words penetrate. We must decide how to integrate faithfulness to him within the context of our economic system. Three possible responses become readily apparent.

One is the easy rationalization which says you must realize that Jesus lived in a very simple agrarian society. He knew nothing of double digit inflation, high interest rates, deficit balance of payments, and commodity markets that can fluctuate erratically. By his own admission, he would have been a poor credit risk. He says, "Foxes have holes and birds of the air have nests, but the Son of Man has no place to lay his head" (Mt. 8:20; Lk. 9:58). Therefore, we surmise, what Jesus has to say about economics cannot be taken too seriously. It's simply not relevant to our modern world. I reject such a rationalization.

A second, but more subtle excuse for shelving Jesus' teaching sounds like this: "Yes, what Jesus had to say about money and economics has worth and truth in it, but the reality of business survival is also real and the two can't really be put together. We just have to be satisfied with a double standard, living as business people six days and as Christians one day a week." This attempt to explain Jesus away I likewise reject.

We are left, then, with the response that attempts to integrate one's faithfulness to Christ with one's situation seven days a week. We think and act the same whether in the marketplace or in the pew—the holy disturbance at work. Obviously this is easier said than done.

A leading agricultural college offered a business seminar for commercial corn farmers. Those farmers in attendance were asked to submit a business profile answering questions such as whether they owned or rented their farm, size of unit, soil type, fertility level of soil, and so on. Near the end of the profile this question appeared: "As a corn farmer do you wish to work six days per week or seven days per week?"

That's a pertinent question in light of the relatively few days available annually to plant corn for maximum yields. In central Illinois corn planted after May 10 experiences progressively lower potential yield per acre. Other considerations indicated by the question include such factors as uncertainty for good planting weather, large dollar investments in machinery, and satisfying the landowner if one is renting. A rational economic case could be made for planting corn seven days a week when the time is right.

One could even rationalize that good stewardship allows for working seven days a week during planting. There may well be more profit dollars available to contribute to the church program.

The question wasn't all that pressing years ago when tired horses needed rest. But today the tractor keeps on running as long as fuel is in the tank. The economic ur-

gency of farming for profit causes one to look enviously at
the successful farmer who is planting seven days a week.
He is my competitor.

At such an intersection between faith and economics
more than a rigid, simplistic legalism is needed. Obviously, some folks, many of them Christians, have jobs
that require them "legitimately" to work on Sunday. The
modern dairy, poultry, or hog farmer does more work in a
few minutes with automated equipment than his
grandfather could have done in a day of hard toil.

What's on the bottom line? "Economics," says profit;
"Christian discipleship," says faithfulness. Two important
considerations surface. The first I refer to as the Sabbath
principle. It calls for a specific part of one's time to be set
apart for worship, adoration, and commitment, away
from the intrusion and concerns of the economic world.

Legalistically, this doesn't have to happen on Sunday
but I believe it must take place regularly. If we fall away
from the worship rhythm, the economic world gains
steadily but surely in relation to our own spiritual life. A
series of small steps in this direction may well lead to
major spiritual compromise. For those whose occupations
may call for Sunday "work," spiritual health would seem
to require that the decision be made within a circle of believers that can call forth spiritual accountability.

A second consideration in the intersection of faith and
economics is illustrated in the biblical account of Jacob
and Esau. Esau, the heir to the spiritual birthright, sold
that spiritual blessing to an enterprising brother for an
economic price, a bowl of soup. In the process, Esau lost
the most important blessing. The New Testament writer
of Hebrews cautions us not to be "godless like Esau, who
for a single meal sold his inheritance rights as the oldest

son" (Heb. 12:16). The lesson stares us in the face: *we dare not put an economic price on spiritual truth.*

The obvious, though not easy, application seems to be that business success cannot be purchased by spiritual compromise without serious consequences in one's relationship with God and the church. More likely than not we will have to bypass some economic opportunities because of the spiritual cost.

I do not believe that profit in business and faithfulness to Christ are mutually exclusive and incompatible, but I do believe that economic decisions should be made in the light of God first. As brothers and sisters in Christ, we take up a faith venture that has meaning for the now and the then. Both in business and discipleship, we face "bottom line" decisions. Where the choices stand in conflict, the one who would follow Jesus has but one choice: faithfulness to our Savior and Lord in the context of Christ's will revealed through the church.

We are called to live with the holy disturbance. As Christians we take courage in claiming Christ's promise of a yoke and a burden that will not be greater than our ability to bear. Praise God!

Time for Reflection

1. If you are part of a study group, share personal experiences of the holy disturbance. What most influenced the outcome?
2. Do you find personal application of the Sabbath principle easy or difficult?
3. A brother in the church owes you $480 for car repairs you did at your garage six months ago. The same pattern has

happened to other business people in town. What do the Scriptures say to that person, to you, to your church?

4. Do you consider yourself rich or poor? Explain your economic status to yourself, your spouse, or a friend; an imaginary South African diamond miner; a person next to you on the plane; God; your study group.

___3. Ever Since Babel___

Now the whole world had one language and a common speech. As men moved eastward, they found a plain in Shinar and settled there.

They said to each other, "Come, let's make bricks and bake them thoroughly." They used brick instead of stone, and tar instead of mortar. Then they said, "Come, let us build ourselves a city, with a tower that reaches to the heavens, so that we may make a name for ourselves and not be scattered over the face of the whole earth."

But the Lord came down to see the city and the tower that the men were building. The Lord said, "If as one people speaking the same language they have begun to do this, then nothing they plan to do will be impossible for them. Come, let us go down and confuse their language so they will not understand each other."

—*Genesis 11:1-7*

God will never allow man to set foot on the moon.
—*Grandma Schertz*

Science discovers, industry applies, man conforms.
—*Motto of 1933 Century of Progress*

With the calm conviction of her Christian faith, my Grandmother Schertz asserted, "God will never allow man to set foot on the moon!" God will not allow it, and

man could never make the long journey, she said. Grandmother Schertz didn't live long enough to see the pictures
of the astronauts walking on the moon or hear their voices
from space. Had she lived that long, her faith would not
have been shaken; she could have handled it. Romans
8:38 and 39 would have brought her through. I praise
God for her faith!

We face the temptation, however, to worship at the
feet of scientific knowledge and technology. We trust
these to free us from anxieties and to provide us with a
long disease-free life lived in ease and comfort. We need
constant reminders that the fruits of science and
technology are to be used in wise stewardship for God's
glory. I am reminded, "The fear of the Lord is the beginning of wisdom" (Ps. 111:10).

One of the most beautiful photographs I have seen
came to us as the astronauts on one of the space missions
turned the camera back toward the earth. We could see
the globe floating in space with clouds of the weather
system clinging to it. That beautiful photo did not show
the suffering, war, and alienation on the earth. Ironically
suffering and wars are made worse by the same
technology that put the space capsule into orbit. Seeing
the earth from outer space causes me to ask with the
psalmist, "What is man?" Contemplation of that question
still causes us to exclaim, "O Lord, our Lord, how majestic is your name in all the earth!" (Ps. 8:1).

The creation account in Genesis 1:6-8 speaks of God
separating the waters above the firmament from the
water below it. My efforts at scientific agriculture look
small by comparison when I realize that each time it rains
one inch on an acre of land, 27,000 gallons of water fall
from heaven. Multiply that one acre many times per

farm, per county, per state, and we get a picture of the
tremendous amount of water needed for plant growth.
Ponder that the next time you water your lawn with a
garden hose!

Six hundred thousand gallons of water per acre are
needed in central Illinois for production of maximum
corn yields. My needed efforts in tillage and fertilization
and related husbandry, look rather puny by comparison.
The photosynthesis process allows one acre of fertile crop
land to produce 150 bushels of corn (8,400 lbs.) from
about 20 pounds of seed. After subtracting the energy
used in production for fuel, fertilizer, and so on, the acre
of land yields a 5 to 1 net energy return. The growing
process releases enough oxygen to meet the requirements
of twelve people for one year and uses enough carbon
dioxide to neutralize the emission from twelve cars and
still improve the organic matter of the soil. Remarkable!

Small wonder God could call the creation good. But
the good creation also becomes a cursed and groaning
creation because of sin. Paul speaks of a groaning creation, subjected to frustration and decay as, along with humankind, it awaits liberation and freedom. These are
meaningful concepts to a farmer steward, conscious of the
environment, ecology, and the pollution, soil erosion, and
abuse being heaped on God's good earth.

Whether by ignorance or design, people in their greed
ignore the fragile balance in the ecosystem—the inter-
relation of animals, plants, and bacteria in a physical and
chemical environment—and use the resources of the
earth as if they were inexhaustible. Technology in the
hands of uncaring humans only accelerates the *entropy* or
depletion of the universe. The psalmist sings: "Of old
thou didst lay the foundation of the earth, and the

heavens are the work of thy hands. They will perish, but thou dost endure; they will all wear out like a garment" (Ps. 102:25-26, RSV).

How we treat creation, whether tenderly as steward managers or as exploiters of a humanly owned commodity, reveals our understanding of God and our relation to the rest of humanity. In my opinion, many Christians blindly accept the assumptions of a culture that has little room for God. Thus, without questioning the end result, we accept as true, that:

> Nature has a virtually infinite storehouse of resources that are there for human use.
> Humanity has the commission to control nature.
> Humanity has the right and obligation to use both renewable and nonrenewable resources for an ongoing improvement in the material standard of living.
> The most effective way to attain individual and social betterment is through the elevation of material standards of living.
> The most effective way to assume the continuing elevation of material standards of living is ongoing economic growth.
> Human failures can be overcome through effective problem-solving. Problem-solving will be effective if reason and goodwill are present and science and technology imaginatively developed and applied.
> Modern science and technology have helped achieve a superior civilization in the West.
> What can be scientifically known and technologically done ought to be known and done.
> The good life is one of productive labor and material well-being.
> The successful person is the achiever.
> The diligent, hardworking, and educated will attain their goals.
>
> —*Birch and Rassmussen, 1978:44f*

We are not only North Americans living in an affluent

capitalistic society. We are also Christians, committed to Christ and our fellow human beings. That should give us a unique view of creation, knowledge, and technology. That view should be one of servant stewards not opportunistic owners. Knowledge and technology will continue to broaden, and wealth may increase. But wisdom will not follow automatically. Technology and capital are easily moved to new places and given new applications, most often resulting in profits but not necessarily in social betterment.

In the early seventies I had the opportunity to visit the Witmarsum Mennonite Colony, near Curitiba, Brazil. I was impressed with the agricultural expertise of the Mennonite farmers. Soybean production, which has since become a major factor in Brazil's economy, was already being practiced successfully by the Mennonites. Yields exceeded those in Illinois.

Since our Mennonite farmer guide could speak only Low German, verbal communication was difficult. So the questions asked in English were translated into Portuguese and then to Low German, then to Portuguese, then to English. In the course of the conversation two words familiar to any Illinois farmer, met my ears. They needed no translation. Those words were TREFLAN, an effective, widely used herbicide for control of grasses in soybeans, and CARGILL, a multinational grain corporation.

Applied technology and investment capital were already working to provide economic profit from new soybean acreages in Brazil. Since then, much land in Brazil has been "cleared" for production agriculture. Through such development, economic wealth has come to some.

But the poor are no better off than before. The soybeans go to the highest bidder on the world market. More soil erodes than previously. The poor are still hungry. Without the direction and motivation to meet human need, technology, knowledge, and investment capital give powerful leverage to the greed and selfishness of individuals and corporate structures. The poor stand naked and helpless. Technology, knowledge, and investment capital also stand naked by themselves and are helpless to change the situation.

How can Christian farmers, whether in Illinois, Iowa, or Brazil, deal with the dilemma? Shall they refuse to use technology or capital wealth? Technology and profits are not dirty words. Hardworking, conscientious farmers work to produce a good product. Soybeans are good food for animals and humans. What should be done differently?

Perhaps one of the most important attitudes in dealing with dilemmas like this is simply to approach life from a servant/steward stance, seeking to serve and share whenever and wherever possible, realizing that we also are a part of "the system." When profits come as a result of invested capital and labor, they should be generously shared. A modest lifestyle also frees more resources to be shared as we consume less according to our perceived needs. There are no easy answers, only difficult choices.

We cannot change economic systems, or stop the exploitation for profit of millions around the world. Only God will effect complete justice and equality. We are called to model the Jesus life and by God's grace become a city set on a hill that will be seen. For some Christians the call will be to opt out of the system, others will strive to be faithful, forced to deal with a great amount of ambiguity. In either case, the call is to bring knowledge and

technology under the lordship of Christ, using the Holy
Spirit to speak new truth through the Word and the community of faith worldwide.

The problems of the world are so large, and the needs
of people so great, that we need a purpose and perspective that keeps us from simply wringing our hands in frustration, or being immobilized by apathy. Such is the effect of the familiar song by Harry Emerson Fosdick:

> Set our feet on lofty places;
> Gird our lives that they may be
> Armored with all Christlike graces
> In the fight to set men free.
> Grant us wisdom, Grant us courage,
> That we fail not men nor thee.
> Save us from weak resignation
> To the evils we deplore;
> Let the search for thy salvation
> Be our glory ever more.
> Grant us wisdom, Grant us courage,
> Serving thee whom we adore.

A visit to Rio de Janeiro, Brazil, helped to give me
needed perspective. Rio is a teeming, bustling city of
great contrasts: wealth and poverty; beautiful beaches
and open sewers; mansions and *favelles* (shantytowns
ringing the city). An Illinois farmer feels lost and alone in
the midst of it. How can the Christian church make an
impact in Rio and in other teeming metropolises of our
world?

Much less, what can a small denomination like the
Mennonites do that will make even the slightest difference? God could take all of the Mennonites in Illinois
and dump them into the middle of Rio, and numerically
we wouldn't even make a ripple. Four thousand among
nine million plus.

But that's not really the question. The question is the same one Jesus asked the disciples as they faced the multitude of 5,000 men plus women and children. I paraphrase Matthew 14:16-20, "Give them something to eat," said Jesus. "We can't," said the disciples. "They are so many; we are so few." "What do you have?" asked Jesus. "Only five loaves and two fish," they replied. The loaves and fish were brought, Jesus gave thanks and broke them, and the disciples gave this food to the crowd. All were fed with twelve basketfuls of broken pieces left over.

We cannot begin to meet all of the world's needs. The needs are beyond our comprehension. We aren't called to meet all of the needs. We are called first in faithfulness in giving what we have.

The question really is, will we be faithful with the loaves and fish in our baskets? Will we dare to believe that God has a way for those who seek his will? God help us!

Time for Reflection

1. Are you comfortable or uncomfortable with the widespread influence of technology? Why?
2. Do you agree with the author that many Christians "blindly accept" cultural assumptions that leave little room for God?
3. What does God desire for the poor in Brazil, Canada, the United States?
4. Name one thing you have done in faithfulness to meet spiritual and human need in your (a) community, (b) nation, (c) world.
5. What are the "loaves and fishes" in your basket?

4. Dominion: Owners or Managers?

O Lord, our Lord,
    how majestic is your name in all
        the earth!

You have set your glory
    above the heavens.
From the lips of children and infants
    you have ordained praise
because of your enemies,
    to silence the foe and the avenger.

When I consider your heavens,
    the work of your fingers,
the moon and the stars,
    which you have set in place,
what is man that you are mindful of
            him,
the son of man that you care for him?
        You made him a little lower than the
                heavenly beings
        and crowned him with glory and
                honor.
You made him ruler over the works of
            your hands;
    you put everything under his feet:
all flocks and herds,
    and the beasts of the field,
the birds of the air,

and the fish of the sea,
all that swim the paths of the seas.
O Lord, our Lord,
how majestic is your name in all
the earth!
—*Psalm 8*

The earth is the Lord's.
—*Psalm 24:1*

The land must not be sold permanently, because the
land is mine and you are but aliens and my tenants.
—*Leviticus 25:23*

We have not inherited the earth from our fathers, we
are borrowing it from our children.
—*Lester Brown*

It's nobody's business what I do with MY land.
—*Farmer*

The human family despite all its pretentions and so-
phistication, despite all its advancements and accomplish-
ments, owes its physical existence on the earth to a thin
layer of topsoil, plus regular amounts of sunshine and
rain.

That thin layer of topsoil, however, is being lost by erosion at an alarming rate. Neglect, ignorance, and poor attitudes about economic ownership are all factors
contributing to the loss of one of God's greatest trusts to
us—the life-giving soil.

The abuse of the soil is only one example of human exploitation of God's creation. I make no apologies for
espousing a conservation ethic. Among others, I point to
three bases for conserving the land.

First, conservation is right. My bias as a Christian supersedes all other reasons. A valid case can be made for conservation from an economic or political perspective. But I believe humankind is entrusted with God's world, to be its steward, manager, caretaker. That means enlightened, sensitive cooperation with nature and not a crushing, destructive kind of self-serving dominion. For me, this reason is basic.

Second, conservation makes for good national and world policy. A growing world population that in many cases lacks safe drinking water, balanced diets, and basic necessities for comfort, can best be served by policies that make the world's resources available to all. Political or economic policies working opposite to these ends cause social unrest, poverty, and war.

Third, conservation is a sustainable systems concept that cooperates with the natural environment. The key word is *sustainable*, for today's depletion of natural resources simply cannot continue at the present rate. Some shrug and say, "Who cares? I'm getting mine now." Some Christians say, "Why worry? The Lord's coming back soon." Our Lord may come soon. We do await Jesus' return, but I also believe that we are to occupy faithfully until the return. That means treating the creation with gentleness and wisdom and conserving resources so that all may share in God's good creation.

Current facts and trends in North American agriculture illustrate the need for commitment to a conservation ethic. Corn is one of the major products of North American agriculture. When grown with proper methods, including conservation practices, corn can capture tremendous amounts of solar energy and return an energy plus of about 5 to 1, at the same time improving the structural composition of the soil as the stover decays and builds up organic matter.

The facts of corn production, however, as presently practiced in North America, don't show the above results. In my state of Illinois where between one and one-and-a-half billion bushels of corn are produced annually, one-and-one-half to two times that many bushels of soil are lost due to water and wind erosion. Two bushels of soil lost for every bushel of corn produced amounts to a grave misuse and loss of a non-replaceable material resource.

This kind of abuse of the creation is a violation both of Christian stewardship and of national wealth. It cannot continue! Voices both in agriculture and the rest of the population must be raised against it. Sadly, soil misuse is only one example of violation against the created universe. Because of a particular economic understanding that legal ownership of private property gives one the right to use that property as one sees fit, some farmers reply, "It's nobody's business what I do with the farm. It's MINE!" Fortunately many Christian farmers disagree with such a statement.

North Americans generally believe that our food is inexpensive in comparison to other areas of the world. Indeed, we do spend a lower percentage of our paychecks for food than almost any other people in the world. It is my contention, though, *that our food* in North America *is not cheap*. The true cost of food must include the deferred costs of soil erosion in addition to the production, distribution, and marketing costs. What does a pound of meat or a gallon of milk really cost when the soil loss costs are added in?

Our system of farm accounting adds to the misconception; it is incorrect and incomplete in its organization and method. I know of no system of farm accounting that takes into consideration the deferred costs of soil loss in determining the economic answer of profit or loss. The truth is that we are selling off the capital wealth of our soils to subsidize our present methods of food production! In accounting terms we are treating capital assets as ordinary income. We are guilty of stealing from God and future generations just as surely as if we were to steal food from the mouths of needy families. These are hard words for me to write—I am a farmer—but they are words that must be heard by both Christians and world citizens.

Again we face a basic question: whose land is it? To whom does it belong? In one sense I can call it mine. The legal title says so. Our economic system allows me to work within the system of private ownership of property. So I speak of "my house, my car, my farm." Many positive things can be said in defense of private ownership, but a real danger exists in that it may block out the fact that "my farm" is also a part of the natural resources of the world.

The production from the farm is a part of the GNP (Gross National Product) of the nation. It represents not only food, but real dollar value influencing international balance of payments between nations. The food produced on "my farm" is also national and international wealth.

But most important for the Christian is the understanding that undergirding the concepts of private and national ownership, and more important than either, is God's ownership. "The earth is the Lord's," declares the psalmist. The land shall not be sold in perpetuity, the land is mine, you are only tenants, God says in Leviticus 25:23. Who really owns the land? My answer to that question will determine in large measure rny attitudes to creation in general, and to resources, limits, conservation, and stewardship in particular.

If the world remains until the year 2000, further serious changes affecting the human family will occur. *The Global 2000 Report to the President,* prepared by the U.S. State Department at the request of President Carter, points up some sobering facts, among them the following:

> Rapid population growth will continue with ninety percent of the growth occurring in the poorest countries.
>
> The large existing gap between the rich and poor nations will widen even further.
>
> Food production will increase but per capita food consumption in lesser developed countries will scarcely improve and in some cases decrease. The real prices for food are expected to double.
>
> Arable land will increase only four percent. Increased production must come from higher yields. Higher yields are heavily dependent on inputs produced from fossil fuels already in short supply.
>
> World forests will decline and the need for available firewood will exceed supplies in a number of areas.
>
> Regional water shortages will become more severe.
>
> Serious deterioration of agricultural soils will occur worldwide due to desertification, salinization, and erosion, loss of organic matter, and waterlogging.
>
> Atmospheric conditions caused by carbon dioxide concentration and ozone depleting chemicals could alter the world's climate. Acid rain from increased combustions of fossil fuels (especially coal) threatens damage to lakes, soils, and crops. Radioactive and other hazardous materials present health and safety problems in an increasing number of countries.

—1981:1-3

The enormity of these problems is almost incomprehensible. They present serious choices for Christians and other world citizens. Short term economic gain should not be sought at the expense of long-term damage to God's creation. We can respond positively, not with handwringing frustration but with real care for the parts of the creation entrusted to our care.

Changes in attitude can take place; I've seen it happen. But positive change follows a well-defined process and usually occurs gradually rather than abruptly. The decision-making process includes five definite steps: identify or become aware of the problem, gather information, weigh the alternatives, take action, conclude with evaluation and modification.

This process has occurred before my own eyes over a fifteen-year period in relation to soil conservation tillage practices. Woodford County, Illinois, is in the middle of the productive corn and soybean belt of Midwest United States. It has rich soils subject to erosion. Conservation tillage as a soil saving measure was introduced about fifteen years ago in a cooperative effort by the county extension agent, the USDA's (United States Department of Agriculture) Soil Conservation Service, and Agriculture Stabilization and Conservation Service.

The concept was tried by some innovators conscious of the need for soil erosion control. Happily, a number of Christian farmers were in the early group of innovators and early adapters. But the idea was greeted with apprehension by most and derision by some. I still remember the verbal barbs, such as, "That's an awful trashy job of farming. Good farmers plow the field black, no stalks showing." But slowly and surely the idea caught on, aided by an almost evangelistic urging by a respected county farm adviser.

Several years ago Woodford County won national recognition as a model of conservation tillage used to control soil erosion. The practice is now used on over 80 percent of the cropland in the county. The idea has moved from the awareness-raising stage with some accompanying derision, to the adoption and modification stage. Some farmers in Woodford County are practicing conservation tillage because social peer pressure now says, "Good farmers don't plow the land black in the fall." Positive change can take place but it takes conviction, repetition, persistence, and time.

The following prayer attributed to Abraham Cowley (1618-67) is a fitting conclusion to this chapter:

> I pray for this:
> To walk humbly on this earth as my father and mother
>   did;
> To greatly love a few:
> To love the earth, to be sparing of what it yields, and not
>   to leave it poorer for my long presence;
> To speak some words in patterns that will be remembered.
> All this, and in some corner where the nettles grew in the
>   black
> soil, to plant and hoe a dozen hills of corn.

Time for Reflection

1. Read Genesis 1:26-31. Explain in your own words the charge given to men and women by God.
2. Do you affirm the three reasons for a conservation ethic listed in the chapter? Why? Why not?
3. List the ways in which private ownership of property has either helped or hindered you to be a better steward manager.
4. What is your Christian response to the *Global 2000* summary?
5. Write a response to Abraham Cowley's prayer; make it your own prayer. "I pray for this. . . ."

5. Settled People in Unsettled Times

When you have eaten and are satisfied, praise the Lord your God for the good land he has given you. Be careful that you do not forget the Lord your God, failing to observe his commands, his laws and his decrees that I am giving you this day. Otherwise, when you eat and are satisfied, when you build fine houses and settle down, and when your herds and flocks grow large and your silver and gold increase and all you have is multiplied, then your heart will become proud and you will forget the Lord your God, who brought you out of Egypt, out of the land of slavery. He led you through the vast and dreadful desert, that thirsty and waterless land, with its venomous snakes and scorpions. He brought you water out of hard rock. He gave you manna to eat in the desert, something your fathers had never known, to humble and to test you so that in the end it might go well with you. You may say to yourself, "My power and the strength of my hands have produced this wealth for me." But remember the Lord your God, for it is he who gives you the ability to produce wealth, and so confirms his covenant, which he swore to your forefathers, as it is today.

If you ever forget the Lord your God and follow other gods and worship and bow down to them, I testify against you today that you will surely be destroyed. Like the nations the Lord destroyed before you, so you will be destroyed for not obeying the Lord your God.

—Deuteronomy 8:10-20

Tell me something new, Dad!
  —*Erik R. Yoder*

Tradition-Tradition-Tradition!
  —*Fiddler on the Roof*

Where your treasure is, there will your heart be also.
  —*Jesus*

In the process of good-natured exchange with my son Erik, he said, with a twinkle in his eye, "Dad, don't always repeat your illustrations. Tell me something new!" Without acting surprised or taken aback, I replied, "I'd like to, son, but you haven't learned the old lessons yet!"

What are some lessons of the past concerning wealth, affluence, and stewardship that would be edifying for us today? Among the many, I mention three:

First, wealth tends to concentrate in fewer and fewer hands. "History records society's response by attempting legislation redistributing wealth or by revolution distributing poverty" (Will and Ariel Durant, 1968:5). The Durants conclude that the concentration of wealth is natural and inevitable, and is periodically alleviated by violent or peaceable partial redistribution.

Second, wide disparity of economic wealth in the church very likely will cause disunity and class consciousness.

Third, political and economic systems are in constant change, sometimes changing rapidly and violently.

The present North American Mennonite scene is marked by great affluence. Is this the expected norm or an exception that cannot last and will probably not be repeated? To what extent is present Mennonite affluence due to our own hard work and to what extent due to being in the right place at the right time?

The perceptive writing of Arnold W. Cressman in the article "When the Big House Is Full" (1980), gives a bird's-eye view of the "Great Frontier" with its economic growth and windfall profits shared by Mennonites in North America. He compares that time with the present which is a different era economically, technologically, and socially, and which is causing basic changes for Mennonites as well as other segments of North American society.

In addition to our hard work and thrift, Mennonites, along with other North Americans, are beneficiaries of a set of circumstances that has allowed us to become the wealthiest people in the world. The geographic frontier with its windfalls is a thing of the past, but much of our present thinking, planning, and actions have not yet taken that into account.

Bruce Birch and Larry Rasmussen list a number of sources of American affluence in their book, *The Predicament of the Prosperous:*

1. A vast virgin continent rich in sources of food, fiber, wood, soil, minerals
2. Millions of immigrants and a century-and-a-half of slave labor
3. Great stores of mineral wealth and fossil fuels
4. A two-ocean moat and a century of cheap national defense
5. A free late start in the industrial revolution
6. Agricultural production
7. Religious, economic, and political doctrines encouraging the exploitation of nature and a cultivation of a competitive spirit.

                              —1978:30ff.

Whether or not one accepts the above statements about our present affluence, we cannot overlook the fast-changing scene in which we find ourselves where material resources are limited, fossil fuels are no longer cheap, people are valued as much by what they consume as by what they produce, and the energy and capital intensive North American industries find that they are losing their competitive edge to foreign producers.

Even our much admired agricultural production has become so capital and energy intensive that it realistically cannot serve as a model for developing nations who have abundant supplies of labor but are limited both in capital and the ability to purchase energy inputs. As a North American farmer I am tempted to point with pride to the fact that one American farmer feeds over seventy people. In reality, however, I only manage purchased inputs that allow me to farm in the present manner.

But I am really depending on the machinery companies, the fuel and fertilizer suppliers, the chemical companies from whom I purchase herbicides and insecticides, and a host of other agricultural suppliers. In real terms I am not as efficient as some of my Asian brother and sister farmers whose *net energy production* in crops is greater and more efficient than mine.

Good stewardship of the creation and its limited resources is already causing many to rethink and redefine "progress and efficiency." I have confidence that North American Mennonites with their ability to innovate and change will use their economic savvy and active faith to produce long-term constructive beneficial changes.

Mennonites find themselves in somewhat the same predicament as the Jewish community depicted in *Fiddler on the Roof*. We similarly are attempting to relate our faith and tradition to a rapidly changing and sometimes unfriendly world. To play the fiddle requires two hands and to sit on the steep roof at the same time takes some doing. What would the Scriptures and our own history teach us concerning economic change?

Moses told the "settled people" on the milk and honey side of the Jordan to take heed. Their nice homes, an expanding economic base of cultivated land, flocks and herds resulted in gold and silver in copious amounts that, coupled with hard work, led the people to say, "Look what we've done!" What God does tends to be overlooked. "You may say to yourself, 'My power and the strength of my hands have produced this wealth for me.' But remember the Lord, your God, for it is he who gives you the ability to produce wealth"

—*Deuteronomy 8:17-18a, see 8:10-20*

The classless shepherd society of Israel from the other side of the Jordan evolved into a class society whom the prophet Amos railed for its injustices and inequalities, and oppression of the poor and widows. The Israel of Amos knew extremes of great luxury, and also great poverty and misery. Israel, in spite of its form of religion, had abandoned true worship to bow down and revel in money, pleasure, and success.

Israel had long forgotten the leveling process of the Jubilee with its forgiveness of debts and repossession of inherited land. The Jubilee principle recognized the natural process of the concentration of wealth into fewer and fewer hands, and was one of God's ways of righting the inequities caused by money and lands kept for selfish purposes and multiplied for personal excesses.

Here's a basic lesson in stewardship for North Americans who make up less than 10 percent of the world's population but who are using up and consuming

resources at a rate far in excess of our needs. We are
among the rich spoken of in the Bible. "Yes, but look how
hard we work, God." The reply comes back now as
before, "The one to whom much is entrusted, from him
much is required."

Coming closer to the present, we should heed the
lessons of the Mennonite experience in Russia, as re-
counted by Mennonite historian C. J. Dyck:

> The beginning of Mennonite life in Russia in late 18th
> century is similar to the end of their organized life as a
> church nearly 200 years later in at least two ways: both
> periods were marked by poverty and suffering, and
> military action decisively helped to shape their destiny. In
> the beginning, poverty and suffering came as natural ac-
> companiments of pioneer life; in the end they came as
> the inevitable lot of refugees.
>
> In a way, the experience of the Mennonites in Russia
> was similar to that of Job when he was stripped of his
> wealth and said, "Naked I came from my mother's
> womb, and naked shall I return; the Lord gave, and the
> Lord has taken away; blessed be the name of the Lord."
> The Mennonites also believed that it was the Lord who
> gave, but they found it a little more difficult to recognize
> Him as the one who also took away.
>
> —*1967:126*

Mennonite sociologist Donavan E. Smucker notes that
in between the beginning and end of the Mennonite
experience in Russia there developed a society with an
economic thrust and wealth not equaled by either the
Dutch or North American Mennonites. The concentration of wealth with its accompanying spiritual coolness
and division allowed many Mennos to become rich and
landed while others became the so-called landless ones.
Large estates of 25,000 acres with 500 horses, 8,000 sheep
and 200 cattle emerged. Dyck (1967) estimates that by

1900 there were 384 large estates totalling approximately 1,000,000 acres. Entrepreneurial vigor was also expressed in business and industry where 2.8 percent of the population owned 75 percent of the total Mennonite capital.

In discussing the Russian Mennonites, Smucker uses two significant words: entrepreneur and *Gelassenheit*. Many of us today can describe the hard working, risk-taking business person, the entrepreneur. But far fewer of us are conversant with Anabaptist *Gelassenheit*, where a person's decisions are made within the circle of the believing community, open to its counsel and insight, tempering one's individual will with group discernment.

Carl Kreider's excellent book, *The Christian Entrepreneur* (1980), presents a positive argument for the possibility of operating in the North American economic system as sensitive, dedicated Christians. I agree with his thesis, but would caution that our past experiences should give us reason for concern, as Donovan Smucker so well says:

> When a disciplined, intelligent people permit unlimited economic expansion, when the juices of free enterprise begin to flow, a highly materialistic civilization develops which can support enormous church sponsored institutions, as well as conspicuous consumption. The setting aside of *Gelassenheit* for the Protestant ethic is the opening wedge for this powerful dynamism. Real human needs are met by the flour of the mills, the implements of the factories, and the credit of the wealthy. But the opening wedge also opens the doors to inequality, dissolution of brotherhood, and resentments which can fuel movements as contrary as communism and counter establishment revivals such as the Mennonite Brethren.
>
> —*1976:231*

Faithful stewardship requires us to learn from the past

and not too easily assume that we are different, that we can handle affluence and wealth. Let us allow the following biblical truths to sink deeply into our lives.

> But godliness with contentment is great gain. For we brought nothing into the world, and we can take nothing out of it. But if we have food and clothing, we will be content with that. People who want to get rich fall into temptation and a trap and into many foolish and harmful desires that plunge men into ruin and destruction. For the love of money is a root of all kinds of evil. Some people, eager for money, have wandered from the faith and pierced themselves with many griefs.
>
> *—1 Timothy 6:6-10*

> Command those who are rich in this present world not to be arrogant nor to put their hope in wealth, which is so uncertain, but to put their hope in God, who richly provides us with everything for our enjoyment. Command them to do good, to be rich in good deeds, and to be generous and willing to share. In this way they will lay up treasure for themselves as a firm foundation for the coming age, so that they may take hold of the life that is truly life.
>
> *—1 Timothy 6:17-19*

I grew up on a 160-acre grain and livestock farm in the community where we still live, in close proximity to the Roanoke Mennonite meetinghouse. Like many Illinois farms in the thirties, dairy cows, hogs, and laying hens supplemented the income from corn sales. Most of the oats raised was fed to the livestock with the horses consuming their share. Tractor power and mechanization of agriculture were just taking hold and the industrialization of agriculture that I experience now was still forty years in the future.

The tasks of corn shelling, hauling the grain by horse and wagon to the rail point, making hay, threshing small

grains, and butchering all required a cooperative neigh-
borhood effort with exchange labor. The neighbors
helped us and we helped them. To refuse a neighbor's
request for help with a task was unthought of because you
needed each other. I can still vividly remember my father
returning home near dark after a hard day's work of helping the neighbors, still needing to face the task of milking
the cows by hand.

Today things have changed dramatically. The farms
are much larger and the fences have been removed to ac-
commodate the large machinery. I now buy the capital
and energy inputs necessary to manage and operate the
farm. Most of the exchange help is also gone. I no longer
need my neighbors economically. They have now become my competitors! The business management adviser
who visits the farm counsels me to rent or buy more land
to increase my efficiency and productivity. Ironically, he
is also advising many other farmers in the county to do
the same. What are the limits of entrepreneural ambi-
tion? How do I know when I've arrived at the boundary
line of wanting to get rich?

"Modern" agricultural economics with an emphasis on
leverage (borrowing) and capital and energy intensive
operating methods that encourage larger and larger units
have increased the competition for land to a fever pitch
that has resulted in farmland being priced far in excess of
its production value. There is more truth than fiction in
the statement, "If you wish to start farming today you
will either need to inherit a farm or marry one!"

Sadly, something much harder to deal with than economic change also confronts me. As I sit in the congregation on Sunday morning and look around, I sometimes
see people not only as brothers and sisters but as business

competitors. How do I deal with that? I know it's real because I've felt it personally. As I've shared this experience across the church, farmers and other business people have told me of their own personal struggle with the same thing.

I'm not about to sell my tractor for a team of horses, or replace the self-propelled combine with a stationary threshing machine. That would only be an avoidance of reality. But I am searching for new ways to cooperate with my neighbors to free both of us from an over-dependence on capital and energy intensive methods.

Most importantly, I need to work more diligently to integrate my spiritual values with economic realities. My own business instincts as an entrepreneur must be kept subservient to the values and spirit of Christ. Business profits and spirit values are not mutually exclusive. But if I must choose between them, the choice is clear. Happily, I am also free to seek out alternatives to farm competition that are as simple and difficult as developing new ways to cooperate and seek the others' welfare as well as my own.

The "bottom line" after all is not economic success. Jesus said it is spiritual faithfulness. May God grant us discernment and courage.

Time for Reflection

1. Use a concordance to find Scriptures that help Christians understand affluence, wealth, poverty, hard work. What impression do these passages make on you?
2. How do the Scriptures you have read apply in areas of the world other than North America?
3. How can the Jubilee principle be applied to our economic life as Christians?

4. What parallels do you note between the Russian Mennonite experience and North American affluence?
5. How can our Christian faith help us to deal with economic change and competition: (a) personally (b) in our congregations?

6. Mennonites and Money: ___Resources or Charity?___

Then Jesus said to his disciples: "Therefore I tell you, do not worry about your life, what you will eat; or about your body, what you will wear. Life is more than food, and the body more than clothes. Consider the ravens: They do not sow or reap, they have no storeroom or barn; yet God feeds them. And how much more valuable you are than birds! Who of you by worrying can add a single hour to his life? Since you cannot do this very little thing, why do you worry about the rest?

Consider how the lilies grow. They do not labor or spin. Yet I tell you, not even Solomon in all his splendor was dressed like one of these. If that is how God clothes the grass of the field, which is here today, and tomorrow is thrown into the fire, how much more will he clothe you, O you of little faith! And do not set your heart on what you will eat or drink; do not worry about it. For the pagan world runs after all such things, and your Father knows that you need them. But see his kingdom, and these things will be given to you as well.

Do not be afraid, little flock, for your Father has been pleased to give you the kingdom. Sell your possessions and give to the poor. Provide purses for yourselves that will not wear out, a treasure in heaven that will not be exhausted, where no thief comes near and no moth destroys. For where your treasure is, there your heart will be also.

—Luke 12:22-34

Fear not, little flock, for it is your Father's good
pleasure to give you the kingdom.
                    —*Luke 12:32, KJV*

The Lord owns my business.
                    —*Common statement*

I want to feel good about the program before I'll commit much of my money.
                    —*Mennonite layman*

What's VS anyway? What do you get out of it?
                    —*Mexican-American*

We have three choices: to live within our means, to attempt living beyond our means, or voluntarily choosing
to live below our means.
                    —*John Rudy, Mennonite Mutual Aid*

First they gave themselves to the Lord and to us by the
will of God.
                    —*2 Corinthians 8:5, RSV*

It matters little whether they are from well-known
Menno-meccas such as Kitchener, Lancaster, Hesston,
Goshen, or Harrisonburg. They may have lesser known
addresses such as Surprise, Arizona; Morson or St. Jacobs,
Ontario; Rheems, Pennsylvania; Tiskilwa, Illinois;
Harper, Kansas; Sugar Creek, Ohio; Guernsey, Saskatch-
ewan; or Bath, New York. I've come to know Mennonites from these and many other addresses as real
spiritual sisters and brothers in the Lord.

People ask about the Mennonite Church: "What is it
like in the various congregations and conferences in
North America?" I'll share four general impressions that
are major ones from my viewpoint:

(1) Mennonites believe deeply that the Bible is the au-
thoritative word of God. Praise the Lord!

(2) There is, however, a lack of consensus as to what the Bible says about a number of vital issues—money and economics being one.

(3) North American Mennonites as a group (with some exception) have become very affluent, and reflect many of the values of the larger society.

(4) Economic stresses are becoming increasingly apparent at personal, business, congregational, and institutional levels.

Hardwork, frugality, innovation, good management, and inflation are just some of the factors that have combined to contribute to Mennonite affluence. Simply to have been placed in North America at a given time in history has already been noted. Some Mennonites, too, would say frankly and honestly that the affluence of many North American brothers and sisters is a direct result of God's blessing on them as good people.

Most Mennonites, however, would raise questions in this regard noting the many sincere, committed Christians here and abroad who are not affluent. They would also affirm, however, that God can and does bless in many ways according to divine will. This may include both economic and spiritual kinds of blessings. In addition to good feelings about affluence, there is also present a real uneasiness and sometimes guilt about money and economic well-being.

It was pointed out in the previous chapter that the lessons of the past are there for our learning and edification. When a people becomes "settled" they have a different economic orientation as compared to refugees or wandering peoples. Well-kept Mennonite farmsteads with silos pointing skyward, fertile fields farmed with loving care according to the latest methods, worship meetinghouses built with the willing offerings of members whose family roots go back several generations in one community all speak of a "settled people." Successful business and professional Mennonites support an institutional structure of mission boards and schools requiring the kind of contribution and offerings that only "settled people" can muster.

A basic question must be raised at this point. Whose money is it that makes possible all of these things? Is it the property of the hardworking Mennonites who are giving some personal wealth to the church as a "charitable" contribution, or is it the Lord's money resources managed by Mennonite stewards that is being designated to a phase of kingdom work? We need to understand stewardship and the difference between it and ownership to appreciate this point. The North American economic system requires us to work within a context of ownership, while the Bible teaches that only God is the owner and we are stewards or managers.

A biblical kind of economic understanding that encourages the faithful management of all resources, recognizing God's ownership and the individuals managerial role, will result in a motivation based on a personal response to God's grace and love as experienced in Jesus Christ. Zacchaeus in the Luke 19:1-10 story offers us such an example.

The late Doris Janzen Longacre called many Christians to new stewardship accountability that included lifestyle issues as an integral part. Her *more-with-less* philosophy has helped thousands of people in North America examine their Christian commitment in a new way.

At one of her numerous workshops I remember her saying that in her early life she didn't take the teachings of Jesus seriously as they concerned wealth and riches because she never thought of herself as rich. Having experienced suffering and poverty in a new way after a term of service in Vietnam, she could only conclude that indeed she was rich by virtue by being a white middle-class North American. We, too, must simply admit that we are among the rich of the world and must not treat the teachings of Jesus as though they apply to others more than ourselves.

Too easily we assume that we can handle and manage wealth and economic resources. Generous gifts of time and money to do not free us from the words of Jesus and Paul: "For the love of money is a root of all kinds of evil" (1 Tim. 6:10). "How hard it is for the rich to enter the kingdom of God! Indeed, it is easier for a camel to go through the eye of a needle than for a rich man to enter the kingdom of God" (Lk. 18:24-25).

I am a rich person relative to most in the world. I also have the desire to be rich when I compare myself with others more wealthy than myself!

Bishop Dom Helder Camera, minister to the poor in Northeast Brazil, said of Jesus' words on wealth:

> Not even you,
> With your irresistible look
> of infinite goodness,
> succeeded in moving
> the heart
> of the rich young man.
> And yet he, from his childhood,
> had kept
> all the commandments.
> Lord, my Lord, may we never,
> out of mistaken charity,
> water down
> the terrible truths
> You have spoken to the rich.
> —*1981:105*

My own stewardship commitment was brought into sharper focus by the testimony of a Voluntary Service leader speaking to our congregation several years ago. His VS unit was located in south Texas among Latinos. In response to questions about the purpose of the VS unit and their reasons for being in the community, VSers related their desire to help in meeting community needs in the context of a Christian commitment.

A question from a local resident to the VS person, however, produced an unexpected lesson in stewardship: "What do you VS people get personally for being here?" The answer given was true, and probably meant to impress the local person with the commitment of the VS people: "Oh we don't get much out of being here—only a place to stay, our food, medical care, and $15 per month." The reply was also true: "Man, what can we do to get a deal like that!"

Even Mennonite Voluntary Service allows us a standard of living beyond the reach and realistic hopes of most people in our world. To admit this to God in humility and repentance is a starting point for our stewardship rather than measuring our commitment in dollars and time contributed. A New Testament based more-with-less attitude is required both out of response to God's love and to the world's great need for compassionate response in the name of Christ. And it is needed on a personal, congregational, conference, and institutional level.

Our response to Christ and the world's need calls for a growing sensitivity and an enlarging stewardship vision. The call for our best commitment of time, talent, and treasures should be kept before us in a number of ways. The helping institutional structures of the church are an attempt to respond in a collective way to meet needs beyond our individual capabilities. Relief agencies, mission boards, church schools, district conference structures, nursing homes, and publishers all play an important part, and all need increasing amounts of resources in funds and personnel.

We must be aware, however, that stewardship and charitable fund raising are not always synonymous. The laws of Canada and the United States allow for charitable tax deductions for contributions that may not meet the test of stewardship. Appeals for funds from within the church must be tested as to kingdom priorities, for the possibility is always present to develop good programs and projects that may well meet the government criteria for charitable deductions taxwise, but may not necessarily further the cause of the kingdom, and may result in larger buildings or programs for our own personal comfort and benefit.

Concentrated efforts to raise funds in large amounts for specific projects may indeed be a legitimate and necessary part of present-day stewardship expression. The important ingredient of a fund-raising effort would be the well-planned opportunity for dialogue within the church as to program balance, priorities, and needs.

A small denomination like the Mennonite Church cannot possibly fund every good program that could be developed and must make choices as to priority. It would be unfortunate if programs would be funded in relation to the most effective fund-raising techniques rather than from steward responses to programs and goals that have broad denominational or congregational testing and affirmation.

Mennonites are a generous people, and dollars con-

tributed per member for church programs local and beyond the congregation generally are higher than for many
other denominational groups in the U.S. and Canada.
Further significant increases will likely result from
increased stewardship conviction and commitment rather
than from traditional or innovative methods of appeal
and fund raising.

The concept of *first fruits resource giving*—giving from
the cream, not the skim milk or whey—is both scriptural
and challenging and would, if understood and practiced,
result in many more committed contributed dollars
available for use in kingdom work. First fruits resource
giving goes beyond the concept of tithing, which is a
good place to start but which is quite inadequate as a
faithful stewardship expression for many affluent North
American Mennonite Christians.

First fruits also goes beyond the "per member asking
goals" which many congregations use to build a budget.
Budgets or giving goals based on per member askings
simply add together mission board, conference, church
schools, and similar "quotas" with local expenses. This
figure then becomes the budget or goal for the coming
year without reference to total resources which might be
available.

First fruits resource giving encourages members to consider the total resources entrusted to them, adopt a personal living budget based on modest lifestyle, and in the
light of faithfulness consider how much of what is already
God's resources they should designate to the church programs. First fruits resource giving also goes beyond a le-
galistic tithe for it would ask of the steward commitment
not only for what is given but also for what is kept and
how it should be used.

I was taught to tithe as a youth. My wife and I have taught our children to tithe. The first fruits tithe is affirmed as a good place to start, but obviously many persons whose incomes can support an affluent lifestyle could give a tithe and still have a large amount of disposable income left over for personal use. Responsible stewardship requires equal consideration for what is kept as well as what is given.

First fruits resource giving incorporates a modest lifestyle that chooses, where possible, a level of consumption lower than one's income would allow and shares in a more generous manner resources to be used in kingdom causes. If the concept of first fruits resource giving would be practiced across the church, much more could be accomplished in Christ's name. The resulting spiritual growth would revolutionize our congregational life and witness.

How much should I give, how much should I invest in savings or business? Can I give when I have money borrowed for business or a house mortgage? What is a modest lifestyle? These questions and many more should be raised in the believing, discerning community of faith. Legalism or pat simplistic answers won't do. But our present inability or unwillingness to openly discuss questions like these in our congregational settings indicates how far we really have to go.

From visiting a large cross section of the church I observe that money and lifestyle issues are among the most difficult for us to discuss. It is probably because these issues are among the most personal ones for us and we feel threatened and vulnerable to open them for discussion.

Business persons may feel alone and appear suspect to

members who simply don't understand the "holy disturbance" and the realities of the balance sheet. Persons of
very modest means may feel a reluctance to share convictions about lifestyle and wealth because of their economic
status. Ministers may feel threatened by wealthy persons
who feel that "pastors just don't know what it's all
about."

Spiritual renewal among us will help to remove these
fears and allow us to begin honest sharing as equal members of the body of Christ. Both the times in which we
live and our confession of faith call for this to happen.

In our economic system the place of production capital
needs to be understood with regard to producing new
wealth and also when and how one contributes funds as a
good steward manager. A business such as a farm requires
a large amount of invested capital in order to operate and
return a hoped-for profit. This needed capital must come
from past savings or profits or must be borrowed at a
price. Obviously, if all profits were given away the business could not continue over a period of time. Those who
work for someone else owe their employment to the fact
that someone has supplied the risk capital necessary to
provide them with a job.

Accumulated capital wealth also needs to be handled
as a stewardship commitment, and the time comes when
either through direct gifts, estate gifts or other methods,
part of it flows directly into the church program. Wise
planning is called for so tax liabilities are minimized. The
excellent services of the Mennonite Foundation and other
Christian estate planners are helpful and needed as
changing situations require expertise beyond the command of most of us.

Disposable income or status wealth needs close scrutiny

for the Christian steward. While important, a simple tithe or 10 percent of disposable income given to the church is only a partial expression of stewardship. How one spends what is left after giving is also important. Here our wants and our needs come into play and lifestyle becomes a testimony of stewardship. Of course, legalism must be avoided in determining how much to give. Some form of resource giving or a graduated tithe—the higher the income the higher the percentage contributed—would seem to be a logical response.

Here again, significant in-depth discernment within the community of faith is needed, for we won't receive the needed help from Wall Street or Madison Avenue. A simple record or budget plan as to how money is spent can be a real help. Firstfruits and overflow can become exciting expressions of faith in a family or personal budget. An excellent tool for helping in this area is Ray and Lillian Bair's record keeping guide, *God's Managers* (1981).

The Mennonite Church General Board action of April 1981 concerning stewardship and fund-raising established a task force to:

A. Review and evaluate the present stewardship services now provided in the Mennonite Church.
B. Propose a stewardship vision for the next five to ten years.
C. Prepare a plan and lines of accountability for carrying out the vision.

The report of the task force underscores that the question of ownership is indeed the critical question: "Is it God's resources or 'our charity?'" The heart of the report is a three-part "call to faithful stewardship":

To All Members of the Mennonite Church

A Call to Gratefully Receive
1. That all members recognize and acknowledge God as the owner and giver of all they are and all they have.

A Call to Faithfully Manage
2. That all members adopt modest standards of living.
3. That all members be good stewards of what money is used (spending, borrowing, investing, saving, insurance, business, etc.)

A Call to Generously Share
4. That all members rediscover and adopt the firstfruits tithe as a minimum standard for proportionate giving.
5. That all members volunteer time and abilities for service in the church at home and/or abroad.
6. That all members plan for the final distribution of their resources by writing wills and including the church along with family members. (See Appendix A for full text.)

How will the Mennonite Church respond to the call to faithful stewardship? I trust we will respond as *steward managers* of God's resources and not as *assumed owners*.

Time for Reflection

1. How should Christians integrate the concepts of legal ownership and divine ownership?
2. What does *more with less* mean to you: (a) as a lifestyle, (b) as to congregational decisions, (c) denominational priorities?
3. What are the firstfruits of your vocation or retirement career? Perhaps you will give testimony of your experience in your group.
4. How can congregations work toward increasing stewardship conviction?

5. Can you affirm the six listed calls to faithful stewardship as a personal faith commitment? How do these calls influence your family life or interaction with close associates?

___7. Facing the Future___

The end of all things is near. Therefore be clear minded and self-controlled so that you can pray. Above all, love each other deeply, because love covers over a multitude of sins. Offer hospitality to one another without grumbling. Each one should use whatever gift he has received to serve others, faithfully administering God's grace in its various forms. If anyone speaks, he should do it as one speaking the very words of God. If anyone serves, he should do it with the strength God provides, so that in all things God may be praised through Jesus Christ. To him be the glory and the power for ever and ever. Amen

—*1 Peter 4:7-11*

Poor little Robert!

—*Grandma Schertz*

When I was a little boy Grandma Schertz loved to hold me on her lap. Often she would look at my mother and say, "How I pity poor little Robert. He's going to grow up in such a sinful, wicked world." Twenty-plus years later my mother held our children. With sincerity she too would say, "Oh how I pity poor little Mike, Susie, Dan, and Erik—growing up in such a sinful world." Now that Doris and I are grandparents, what should we say about our grandchildren, the world, and the future?

Paul's statement to Timothy that the last days will be times of terrible stress (2 Tim. 3:1) is true, not because people are inherently more evil than any other time in history, but because the leverage of exploding technology and knowledge and wealth give people more influence and power over others.

I believe the community of faith forms the greatest reality for us as Christians and for our children and grandchildren. Here together we worship God, confess Jesus as Lord, pray and praise, and receive strength with those of our primary peer group, fellow members of Christ's body. We confidently encounter our world as faithful stewards in the name of the one who said, "Be of good cheer. I have overcome the world."

Today the church of Christ worldwide finds itself in varied and rapidly changing situations. We can expect that change will continue to accelerate. The stewardship of the gospel entrusted to us is not dependent on a given economic or political system for survival or propagation. Rather the first call to the steward is to be faithful. Wisdom also calls for endurance and flexibility. Further, I believe that we are called to reactivate and redefine a stereotyped word in the Mennonite vocabulary—*nonconformity*. Ron Sider says:

> Biblical revelation summons us to defy many of the basic values of our materialistic, adulterous society. The values of our affluent society seep slowly and subtly into our hearts and minds. The only way to defy them is to immerse ourselves deeply in Christian fellowship so that God can fundamentally remold our thinking as we find our primary identity with other brothers and sisters who are also unconditionally committed to biblical values.
>
> *(1977:190)*

Sociologically we become a cognitive minority, people who hold values in sharp contrast to society and who know why we do. Through the power of Christ, we become stewards of God's grace in our world. Pastor Harvey Yoder of Broadway, Virginia, has said, "Nonconformity doesn't mean being so far behind the times that you are strange and different. It means being so far ahead of the times that you may seem strange and threatening."

Elton Trueblood adds to the perspective. We need Christian intellectuals, he says, who are tough-minded and tenderhearted. These Christians, he says, must think with their minds and pray and love with their hearts. They are ones "who are unabashed and unapologetic in the face of opposition and ridicule. They must be able to outthink as well as outlive all attacks on the central faith which we so sorely need as an alternative to confusion" (1969:20). With access to both the "reasons of the heart and the reasons of the head," the Christian intellectual has "both intellectual integrity and depth of experience. In short, he can both pray and think!" (31f.) Trueblood maintains that there need be no quarrel between clear-mindedness and reverence. We can be intellectually honest and spiritually true in our nonconformity.

We must be neither unduly pessimistic nor optimistic about facing the future. The pessimist says, "It's no use, nothing I can do will matter," while the optimist glibly says, "Why worry, it will all come out okay in the end." Christ calls for us to become extensions of his love and concern. That requires our best commitment and management of time, talent, and treasure. To seek first the kingdom, to live as citizens of the kingdom, and to invite others into God's kingdom is the objective of our stewardship commitment.

In chapter 6 I mentioned the seeming lack of a Mennonite consensus concerning money and economics. Noted also was the fact that economic stresses are present at every level of church structure from individual to institutional. This includes differences as to funding and policymaking procedures.

Competition for available funds is becoming more intense. How should denominational priorities be determined and programs supported? How can a denomination that is congregational by definition and practice develop and support necessary helping institutional structures? On the personal level, political and economic bias cloud a good many discussions carried on within the church and cause polarization and disunity. These and other kinds of issues will become more intense and pose serious threats to real community.

The passage from 1 Peter 4:7-11, one of the familiar stewardship passages of the New Testament, includes this admonition: "Above all, love each other deeply, because love covers a multitude of sins" (8). As we search together for meaningful expressions of stewardship commitment in the years ahead, this word of truth will instruct us repeatedly. Within the believers' church, with lots of give and take and differences of opinion, it is likely that persons may get hurt in the process. Indeed some of our best and worst experiences may take place in the church.

Forces and circumstances not of our choosing will continue to be thrust upon us, causing us to count the cost of discipleship. Economic, political, and technological advance will continue to cause basic change in our way of life because "the big house is full" (Cressman, 1980).

Nuclear threat, uncertain international monetary policies, the needs of the Third World are only a few of the realities that make this a "Jeremiah time," a time to be realistic about the present dangers, but also to be hopeful enough to buy a field. It is a time when the church must not yield to the temptation of short-term expediency at the expense of long-term effectiveness. We must not stop planting the slow-growing sturdy oak trees in favor of the fast-growing willow shoots. Faithfulness and flexibility are watchwords for us.

Our Lord has told us through the Scriptures that the faithful and wise steward manager is the one who faithfully goes on doing the Master's bidding while awaiting the Master's return. We should not be unaware, however, that doing our Master's bidding involves a testing by fire that may cause division reaching even into close family circles (Lk. 12:49-53). But faithful stewardship brings with it the reward of the Master and a yoke that is easy and a burden that is light.

The Mennonites of North America have become a "settled people" economically and culturally. We are at home here. Can we have the mind-set of a pilgrim people in relation to the changing times in which we live? With thankfulness and humility for the blessings of the past and present, we can confidently, full of hope, anticipate the future. Our practice of Christian stewardship will keep our eyes fixed on the kingdom.

Today we hear the all inclusive charge to consecrate the entrusted resources of time, talent, treasures, and life itself in faithful stewardship to the one who is, who was, and who is to come, the Alpha and the Omega, God Almighty.

Time for Reflection

1. Identify your spiritual gift(s).
2. How are you using your gift(s) as a steward for God's glory?
3. Where do you find your most trusted peers—(a) church, (b) business world, (c) other?
4. Do you agree that nonconformity is an important value? How do you apply it?
5. How has what you mean by stewardship changed since you began to read this book? Write down the goals you want to meet short- and long-range as a faithful steward manager who has received God's gift in Jesus Christ.

_____

_____

_____

_____

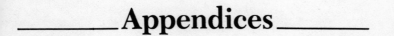

Appendices

Appendix A

A Call to Faithful Stewardship
Mennonite Church General Board

To All Members of the Mennonite Church

PREAMBLE

As Christians we believe that we are called to follow Christ in a life of discipleship and that a significant part of that discipleship is a faithful use of all of the resources of which God has made us stewards. We believe that these resources as well as our lives are entrusted to us to use for the glory of God, for the furtherance of his kingdom, and for the benefit of others.

This call to faithful stewardship recognizes the pressures of our world to influence Christians to conform to its materialistic, accumulative, and consumptive values. Thus there is a need for the church to call Christians to live by the teachings of Christ and his Word as faithful stewards.

This call to faithful stewardship also recognizes the pioneering work of Milo Kauffman and Dan Kauffman by whose efforts the church has been enriched in its understanding of stewardship teaching and methods. The present ministries of churchwide staff persons are helping the church to grow in its stewardship practices.

This is a call to the Mennonite Church to give special attention to faithful stewardship in the following ways:

A CALL TO GRATEFULLY RECEIVE
1. That all members recognize and acknowledge God as the owner and giver of all they are and all they have.

A CALL TO FAITHFULLY MANAGE
2. That all members adopt modest standards of living.
3. That all members be good stewards of what money is used (spending, borrowing, investing, saving, insurance, business, etc.)

A CALL TO GENEROUSLY SHARE
"Firstfruits 10 Plus"
4. That all members rediscover and adopt the firstfruits tithe as a minimum standard for proportionate giving.
5. That all members volunteer time and abilities for service in the church at home and/or abroad.
6. That all members plan for the final distribution of their resources by writing wills and including the church along with family members.

Recommendations to Boards, Agencies, Conferences, and Congregations
A. General Board
1. That Board members and staff be an example to the church by making a commitment to practice "A Call to Faithful Stewardship."
2. That the General Board establish denominational priorities for the use of Mennonite Church resources.
3. That the General Board promote a churchwide emphasis and awakening to stewardship and accountable use of resources.
4. That the General Board establish a Churchwide Stewardship Council.

5. That the General Board call for MBCM and the conferences to give more careful attention to the financial needs of pastors and to plan carefully for retirement needs.

B. Churchwide Agencies
1. That Board members and staff be an example to the church by making a commitment to practice "A Call to Faithful Stewardship."
2. Seek ways to support, nourish, and facilitate the church's program at the congregational level as well as operate churchwide programs in behalf of the denomination.
3. Have a contingency budget for operating at reduced income in the event of severe economic recession.
4. Find more ways to use the volunteer services of the constituency to accomplish the mission of the church.
5. Find ways to terminate programs and services that are no longer needed and are being duplicated by the conferences, so that finances can be released to begin new programs.
6. Implement ways to demonstrate good stewardship in the employment and management of resources.
7. That college Bible courses and seminary curricula include teaching in the biblical principles and practical applications of Christian stewardship.

C. Conferences
1. That conference officers and staff be an example to the church by making a commitment to practice "A Call to Faithful Stewardship."
2. To examine with congregations the financial needs of pastors and to plan for their retirement needs.
3. To evaluate with congregations the amount of money spent in the home program to see that it is for congregational mission and service, and not merely for "comfort."
4. To encourage congregations to keep capital expenditures in balance with mission and service program expenditures.

5. To give attention to stewardship education in the congregations.
6. To participate in the Churchwide Stewardship Council by appointing a Conference Stewardship Secretary.
7. To suggest to congregations that they allow plenty of room for designated giving in the administration of unified budgets.
8. To commend individuals and congregations for generous giving.
9. To give attention and encouragement to congregations for supporting the programs of the churchwide boards and agencies.

D. Congregations
1. That pastors/elders/other leaders be an example to the congregation by making a commitment to practice "A Call to Faithful Stewardship."
2. That congregational leaders give careful attention to the financial needs and the retirement planning for the pastor.
3. To evaluate the amount of resources invested in the home program to see that it is for congregational mission and service, and not for mere "comfort."
4. To keep capital expenditure in an appropriate balance with mission and service expenditures.
5. To give attention to stewardship education.
6. To allow freedom for designated giving in the administration of unified budgets.
7. To encourage support for and participation in conference and churchwide programs.
8. To encourage and command members for generous giving.
9. To give attention to financial needs of members.

Appendix B

Christian Stewardship: The Real World

by John H. Rudy

Suggestions for making Christian stewardship practical in your daily life

1. Share your Christian faith as a good steward of the gospel.
2. Dedicate time and abilities to voluntary service in the mission of the church, at home, and/or abroad.
3. Work hard in a vocation which allows you to provide helpful products and services to society.
4. Adhere to a responsible standard of living which symbolizes and demonstrates your life in Christ.
5. Adopt practices which help preserve natural resources such as farmland and energy.
6. Control your spending and consumption by use of a budget or other workable method.
7. Exercise extreme caution in the use of credit.
8. Use sound judgment and faith in the purchase of insurance.
9. Invest your savings prudently and in harmony with your Christian beliefs.
10. Give a proportionate share of your income to church causes beginning with the firstfruits tithe.
11. Make sure your charitable contributions are going to worthy causes.

12. See that charity begins at home by helping your children when they need it the most.
13. Teach Christian values and good money management to your children.
14. Help needy persons even though your gifts may not qualify for income-tax deductions.
15. Participate in mutual aid which helps provide for the needs of Christian brothers and sisters.
16. Find effective ways to help persons who are suffering unemployment, financial distress, or business failure.
17. Maintain an up-to-date will which provides for your family and includes the work of the Lord.
18. Seek competent estate planning counsel when your estate requires analysis.
19. Use legal methods to minimize your taxes as you attempt to pay your fair share.
20. Keep good records and make sure your family knows where all your important papers are located.
21. Abstain from substances which are harmful to your physical and mental well-being.
22. Adopt safe driving practices which preserve life and property.
23. Avoid gambling, lotteries, and other practices which waste resources.
24. Refuse to let differences in wealth and income become obstacles to Christian fellowship.
25. Stay in touch with counselors who can help you achieve your Christian and financial objectives.
26. Enter actively into the congregational decision-making processes of budgeting.
27. Remain open to brotherly and sisterly guidance and admonition.

Appendix C

When the Big House Is Full

by Arnold W. Cressman

It is now becoming clear, even to the casual observer, that we are entering a different era. There is no consensus among the prophets on what will take shape or how. They are agreed only that the door to the world, as we have known it, is closing. If anyone has doubts about it, he need only look around at the freshly cut piles of firewood, or the widespread prospect of reduced expectations. There is a deep-set unease about the state of the economy. The more perceptive persons sense that a surface fix will no longer be enough.

What we need desperately is a larger perspective. Could it be that the constant-unlimited-growth world we have known for 200 years is not the real world after all? How can a broader and a longer perspective be made to help?

One of my jobs as a youngster on the farm at New Hamburg, Ontario, was to fetch the cows in the evening. In the fall of the year the herd had free range over 164 acres. Which direction should one go to start looking? The wisest course was to climb the windmill. From that perspective the cows could not hide in the fold of any hill. You could walk directly to them, even if they had found some unusual corner of a field. Perspective made the difference.

Would you climb a windmill with me to see whether or not we are reaching the end of an era? We will need to climb high enough to see back to year 1500 and to see half the globe at once.

Europe, AD 1500, from this perspective was a single community. Walter Prescott Webb, in his book *The Great Frontier*, calls it "the Metropolis." Lines between countries and principalities were largely irrelevant because the culture, the religious system, and the economy had all flowed together. The population in "the Metropolis" was roughly 100,000,000 and had held that level for a full three hundred years. They had what we would now call a "steady state" economy. There was no growth and no one expected any. At 26.7 people per square mile, the "Little House" of the Metropolis was full. People had to cooperate to survive. Garrett Harden's apt figure makes the point. If "the commons," an open land area, was large enough for ten families each to graze exactly ten cows, then one family adding one additional cow would deprive all the other families by a little. When the field was full the cow owners had to cooperate.

Suddenly something changed! Word flashed through the Metropolis that Columbus had discovered a vast new land. It was an electrifying message! An empty continent with fabulous resources was suddenly accessible. In rapid succession other frontiers emerged out of nowhere—South America, Australia, New Zealand, South Africa. The people of the Metropolis, whose house had been full now had a 500 percent increase in available land. And the flow of wealth began. Spanish galleons, which had successfully eluded the buccaneers, came home heavily laden with gold and silver. Timber and furs in abundance arrived, as well as new crops, exotic foods, and optimism beyond measure. All this quickly fueled the economy of the Metropolis. It upset the three hundred-year equilibrium. The steady-state economy turned to growth.

What of the little man in the Little House? For three hundred years, and longer, he had been a nobody. He blended well with the drab grayness of peasantry. He was dirt poor, deeply in debt, hopeless, circumvented by laws, rules, and restrictions. He was surrounded by standing institutions un-changeable as the hills. The little man saw a stratified society. He knew his place at the bottom of it. He was powerless to move up even one rung on the ladder of success. Individualism had not yet been invented, so the little man was really an insig-nificant piece blended into the corporate identity. He was nothing alone. Even his sins could hardly be forgiven unless he scraped up money to pay the priest.

The word about the frontier spread like a prairie fire before the breeze. Here was opportunity, here was hope for the little man. Here was the beginning of a new era. In the new land one could stake a claim, get land, get wealth, be independent! With a title deed to 200 acres no one could tell the little man that he was not of the bourgeoisie. He was somebody. It was in his soul. Best of all for the little man now getting big were the many freedoms the new era brought.

Now, in an empty land, there was the promise of freedom from restriction, freedom from the oppressive church, freedom from locked-in stratification, freedom from poverty and from debt, freedom from illiteracy, freedom to think new thoughts, and freedom to be a person, an individual.

Ah, but each of those freedoms also harbored the seeds of destructive individualism. And individualism could be tolerated only when the house was less than full. It might be noted that America's first settlers were mostly those who were running away—from staid religion, from debt, or from persecution. These persons were grateful to be free. They had little interest in noting the dangers of individualism.

A brief sketch of the religious scene in Europe in terms of its contribution to the rise of individualism might be helpful.

Erasmus, the sixteenth-century Dutch theologian and hu-manist, helped people to see the worth of individuals.

John Calvin added a theology to what people were about to do anyway. He said basically that God likes you if you produce. Prosperity then proved that you were predestined for heaven. And the work ethic was well underway.

Martin Luther emphasized individual salvation, that one is saved by "faith alone" thus deemphasizing the importance of the church, the gathered community.

Ulrich Zwingli affirmed the worth of the common man by preaching directly from the Bible to all who would come to hear him at the Gross Munster in Zurich.

The Anabaptists noted that adult individuals could say "yes" or "no" to Jesus, that baptism would verify an adult individual choice, but that this should all be done in the context of the church, the brotherhood. Even the Scriptures were to be interpreted in community.

Here, at the earliest stage of the movement of the Swiss Brethren, we have a people who did not fit into the emerging status quo. They accepted persons as individuals but they objected to individualism by insisting on brotherhood as the best expression of the church.

The radicalness of such a brotherhood, in the context of the times, can hardly be overemphasized. On the one hand, in the old order, people knew their place; on the other, in the emerging order, individualism was being affirmed on all sides. In this uneasy mix, the Anabaptists were showing that a Christian brotherhood could gather up the multiple individualities and make of the church a corporate whole as the epistle to the Ephesians describes it.

Note, then, the rapid growth of individualism. The genie had been let out of the bottle. What would happen now? The newly invented individualism had its greatest opportunity in America. Follow the pioneer into the slowly receding frontier. Compare this individualist to the little man, his earlier brother, in Europe. The pioneer could cut down a tree, dam up a stream, ride the range, make his own laws, and flash his Colt revolver to see that they were obeyed. He was a lone ranger; he could stake a claim, pan for gold, shoot a hundred buffalo, and increase his herd of longhorns. He was self-reliant. There were few to help and less to hinder him. Here was freedom! Here was individualism because the "Big House" was empty.

In the early days of the new nation all systems affirmed the newly invented individualist. Jonathan Edwards, the eighteenth-century theologian and preacher, carried the Calvinistic religious banner. Hardly anything could have affirmed individualism more than Edwards did in his fearful sermon, "Sinners (individuals) in the Hands of an Angry God." Politically, the new Declaration of Independence promised "unalienable rights" which seemed perfectly obvious to the drafters—life, liberty, and the pursuit of (individual) happiness. The social maxims of Ben Franklin affirmed the pursuit of individual greed, which was usually mistaken for happiness: "early to bed, early to rise makes a man healthy, wealthy, and wise" or "a penny saved is a penny earned" or "God helps those who help themselves." The new laissez-faire philosophy affirmed with a straight face that it is best for the economy if everyone is free to pursue individual goals because competition is good and the "Invisible Hand" will balance things out for the good of all.

It is obvious now that laissez-faire can work only when the "house" is largely empty, but nobody needed to think those thoughts then. So work was glorified. There was unlimited opportunity. And the impractical idea of "constant-unlimited-economic-growth" was internalized in a single, unhesitating gulp. Much later the insightful Walter Prescott Webb observed that if you have resources, land, and opportunity in seemingly unlimited quantities then the work ethic will invent itself simply because of man's insatiable greed.

This rapid survey serves to show that, when North America was young, we had a rapidly rising tide of individualism. It was the dominant mood of the fledgling country. It was the spirit of the age. It was the carefully modeled ideal for the young in schoolbooks, in parents, and in the pulpit.

It is 1683. The atmosphere is bristling with vigor. All the individuals are in pursuit of something—politically it is the pursuit of happiness, economically it is the pursuit of greed, religiously it is the pursuit of individual salvation. In the middle of all this a small group of Mennonites and Quakers, fresh from

Europe, settled at Germantown, Pennsylvania, six miles north of the one-year-old town of Philadelphia. A people whose theological treasure was *brotherhood* stepped into the rising tide of enthusiastic individualism!

What happens to a tiny religious minority when they learn that their theology is sharply out of tune with the whole orchestra? In short, the situation was this. Anabaptist/Mennonites whose theology was born as something of a corrective to emerging individualism in Europe found themselves in a new land just as individualism burst forth unchallenged. What was there for a Mennonite to do but to shoulder an ax, stake a claim, cut out a farm like all the other entrepreneurs. If he worked hard, he could rise to the middle-class landholding level just as the new laissez-faire philosophy said he could. The system worked! On the short run it worked. The Big House was still empty.

Given the flood of individualism that surrounded Mennonites from day one when they arrived in America, is it any wonder that their theology began to be bent toward the rising sun of a new mood? Many Mennonites today have never noticed that the church, the basic brotherhood, is wholly missing in many of the songs they love to sing like: "My God and I Walk Through the Fields Together" or "I'm But a Stranger Here," or "What Can Wash Away My Sins?" It is amazing, given the contingencies, that brotherhood remained alive at all!

Now a new situation is upon us. The tide is turning. We are in the 1980s and the Big House is getting full. In 1930 the Big House reached a population level of 27 people per square mile (Webb) the same as the 1500 population level was for the Little House. By 1950 it had reached 34 per square mile and it has grown since. The frontier is finished. Not one of the new frontiers postulated by politicians has a magnitude anywhere near the order of the one that has just evaporated. Instead, since the great frontier is gone and as the tide of individualism recedes, we can see its effects. Individualism
—has raped the good land.

—has poisoned the fresh air.

—has polluted the sparkling water.

—has set man against his neighbor and against nature. Government must step in or strip miners will not backfill the mines, factories will not put scrubbers on their stacks, auto makers will not make safe cars, and Three Mile Islanders will not tell how much radiation has leaked out during the accident.

Happily, there are quiet signals of cooperation coming both from voluntary action groups and from the law courts. There are food co-ops and car pools, equipment is being shared, townhouses are being built instead of one-family units on half-acre lots, communal living is becoming more attractive. And now, of all things, management and labor in some companies are cooperating to hold down wages in order to save those companies. Cooperation is descending upon us because the Big House is nearly filled. A clear signal that the old era with its seemingly limitless resources is ending is the sharp rise in the price of oil. When 1973 two-dollar-per-barrel oil cost $30-40 in 1980, then only the economically blind can expect all things to continue in the world as they were. The days of throwaway flashlights and disposable razors are nearly over. Planned obsolescence will soon be a sin against society. When the Big House is full, each person's share will be limited and all must learn the meaning of the word "cooperate."

It happens that the theological counterpart to the word "cooperation" is "brotherliness." We Mennonites can say, "That is our word." John L. Ruth pointed out at a Laurelville Mennonite Church Center Symposium in 1978 that Mennonites should learn to give what they have to their world. He offered two items from their heritage, obedience (discipleship) and humility. Let's add "brotherliness." We have not really lost it in spite of the pressures.

Suppose all the Mennonites would go up to their ancestral attics, sort around a bit, find their treasured brotherliness, dust it off, and bring it out to the light of day. Suppose they would begin modeling the very thing that is now sorely needed in the decade of frugality that is ahead for all of us. Suppose we would quietly show how a people can live together in peace, in shalom, even when the Big House is finally full.

If a Bible verse can help us to do what we should do anyway, it might be the questioning words of Mordecai to Queen Esther, "Who knows but that you are called to the kingdom for such a time as this?" (Esther 4:14c).

—Reprinted by permission of the author from *Gospel Herald* (April 8, \
1980). For a more comprehensive review of the historical developments that have brought us to a full Big House, read *The Great Frontier* by Walter Prescott Webb (Austin: University of Texas Press, 1979).

____References Cited____

BAIR, Lillian and Ray
1981   *God's Managers*. A budget guide and daily financial
       record book for Christians. Scottdale, Pa.: Herald Press.

BIRCH, Bruce and RASSMUSSEN, Larry
1978   *The Predicament of the Prosperous*. Philadelphia:
       Westminster Press.

CRESSMAN, Arnold
1980   "When the Big House Is Full," *Gospel Herald* (April 8)

DURANT, Will and Ariel
1968   *The Lessons of History*. New York: Simon and Schuster,
       Inc.

DYCK, C. J. (ed.)
1967   *Introduction to Mennonite History*. Scottdale, Pa.:
       Herald Press.

SIDER, Ronald J.
1977   *Rich Christians in an Age of Hunger*. Downers Grove,
       Ill.: InterVarsity Press.

SMUCKER, Donovan
1976   "Gelassenheit, Entrepreneurs, and Remnants: Socioeco-
       nomic Models Among the Mennonites," in *Kingdom,
       Cross, and Community*, edited by John Richard
       Burkholder and Calvin Redekop. Scottdale, Pa.: Herald
       Press.

TRUEBLOOD, Elton
1969   *A Place to Stand.* New York: Harper and Row.

UNITED STATES GOVERNMENT
1980   *Global 2000 Report to the President, Summary.* Wash-
       ington, D.C.: Government Printing Office.

_____ Bibliography _____

BAIR, Lillian and Ray
1981   *God's Managers:* a budget guide and daily financial record book for Christians. Scottdale, Pa.: Herald Press.

BIRCH, Bruce and RASSMUSSEN, Larry
1978   *The Predicament of the Prosperous.* Philadelphia: Westminster Press.

BROWN, Lester
1981   *Building a Sustainable Society.* New York: Norton/ World Watch.

BRUEGGEMANN, Walter
1976   *Living Toward a Vision.* Philadelphia: United Church Press.
1977   *The Land.* Philadelphia: Fortress Press.
1982   "The Bible: Resource for Speaking to the World Around Us." Tape of Address at Associated Mennonite Biblical Seminaries.

BURKHOLDER, Richard and REDEKOP, Calvin (eds.)
1976   *Kingdom, Cross, and Community.* Scottdale, Pa.: Herald Press.

CAMERA, Dom Helder
1981   A *Thousand Reasons for Living*. Philadelphia: Fortress
       Press.

Catholic Bishops' Statement on Land Issues
1980   *Strangers and Guests*. Sioux Falls, S.D.: Heartland
       Project.

DESANTO, Charles P., REDEKOP, Calvin, and SMITH-
       HINDS, William L. (eds.)
1980   A *Reader in Sociology: Christian Perspectives*. Scott-
       dale, Pa.: Herald Press.

DURANT, Will and Ariel
1968   *The Lessons of History*. New York: Simon and Schuster,
       Inc.

DYCK, C. J. (ed.)
1967   *Introduction to Mennonite History*. Scottdale, Pa.:
       Herald Press.

EBY, John and NELSON, Boyd
1976   "The Institutionalization of the Church" in *Mission
       Focus*, Elkhart, Ind.: Mennonite Board of Missions.

ERB, Paul
1955   *The Alpha and the Omega*. Scottdale, Pa.: Herald Press.

FAIRFIELD, James H. T.
1977   *All That We Are We Give*. Scottdale, Pa.: Herald Press.

FISHER, Wallace E.
1979   *All the Good Gifts*. Minneapolis: Augsburg.

FOSTER, Richard J.
1978   *Celebration of Discipline*. San Francisco: Harper and Row.

GHEDDO, Piero
1973   *Why Is the Third World Poor?* New York: Maryknoll:
        Orbis.

HATFIELD, Mark
1976   *Between a Rock and a Hard Place.* Waco, Texas: Word.

HESS, J. Daniel
1977   *Ethics in Business and Labor.* Scottdale, Pa.: Herald
        Press.

KAUFFMAN, Daniel and RUDY, John
1981   *A Congregational Guidebook in Money and Economic
        Issues.* Goshen, Indiana: Mennonite Mutual Aid.

KAUFFMAN, Milo
1975   *Stewards of God.* Scottdale, Pa.: Herald Press.

KRAYBILL, Donald B.
1978   *The Upside-Down Kingdom.* Scottdale, Pa.: Herald
        Press.

KREIDER, Carl
1980   *The Christian Entrepreneur.* Scottdale, Pa.: Herald
        Press.

MARTIN, Jason
1977   *The People of God in Community.* Scottdale, Pa.: Men-
        nonite Publishing House.

NEUFELD, Dietrich
1977   *A Russian Dance of Death: Revolution and Civil War in
        the Ukraine.* Translated by Al Reimer. Winnipeg, Man.:
        Hyperion Press; Scottdale, Pa.: Herald Press.

RASMUSSEN, Larry L.
1981   *Economic Anxiety and Christian Faith.* Minneapolis:
        Augsburg.

REDEKOP, Calvin
1970   *The Free Church and Seductive Culture.* Scottdale, Pa.:
        Herald Press.

RIFKIN, Jeremy
1980   *Entropy.* New York: Viking.

RIFKIN, Jeremy and HOWARD, Ted
1979   *The Emerging Order.* New York: Putnam.

SCHUMACHER, E. F.
1973   *Small Is Beautiful.* New York: Harper and Row.

SIDER, Ronald J.
1977   *Rich Christians in an Age of Hunger.* Downers Grove,
        Ill.: InterVarsity Press.

SNYDER, Howard A.
1977   *The Community of the King.* Downers Grove, Ill.: In-
        terVarsity Press.
1975   *The Problem of Wineskins.* Downers Grove, Ill.: Inter-
        Varsity Press.

TAYLOR, John V.
1975   *Enough Is Enough?* Minneapolis: Augsburg.

TRUEBLOOD, Elton
1969   *A Place to Stand.* New York: Harper and Row.

UNITED STATES GOVERNMENT
1981   Department of Agriculture. *Summary Report on the*

Structure of U.S. Agriculture. Washington, D.C.: Government Printing Office.

1980 *Global 2000 Report to the President, Summary.* Washington, D.C.: Government Printing Office.

WALLIS, Jim
1981 *The Call to Conversion.* San Francisco: Harper and Row.

WEBB, Walter Prescott
1951 *The Great Frontier.* Austin, Tex.: University of Texas Press.